This Book Belongs To